HANUKKAH
The Festival of Lights

Hanukkah is a Jewish celebration also known as "The Festival of Lights." It begins on the twenty-fifth day of the Hebrew month of Kislev, usually in November or December, and lasts for eight days. During Hanukkah, Jewish people celebrate the victory of a group of Jewish soldiers a long time ago. After that victory, the soldiers began to clean and rebuild the temple in Jerusalem so they could worship there again. They searched for oil to light a special lamp, but found only enough oil to last one night. Miraculously, the oil lamp burned for eight days!

Today, Hanukkah is celebrated with specially prepared foods, traditional songs, and gift-giving. A four-sided top called a dreidel is used to play a traditional game, and families light candles on a special nine-branched candle holder called a menorah.

Make a dreidel and play this popular Hanukkah game.

How to make a dreidel:

Wash and clean an empty half-pint milk carton. Have an adult use scissors or a craft knife to make a small hole in the bottom of the carton. Slide a pencil through the top of the carton and the bottom hole, then staple or tape the top closed. Cut out the Hebrew letters on page 3 and glue them to the sides of the milk carton clockwise in this order: Shin, Hey, Gimmel, Nun. While the glue dries, carefully color and cut out the gelt pieces on page 3 and save them in an envelope until you are ready to play.

How to play dreidel:

Sit in a circle with a small group of friends. Divide the gelt pieces equally between all players. Each player puts one gelt piece in the middle. Take turns spinning the dreidel. Follow the directions below, based on which Hebrew letter appears on top:

Shin—Share your gelt. Put one gelt piece in the middle.

Hey—Take half the gelt from the middle.

Gimmel—Take all the gelt from the middle. Players each put one piece in the middle.

Nun—Do nothing. Let the next player spin.

A player is out when she loses all of her gelt pieces. The game ends when one player wins all of the gelt.

Use these patterns and gelt pieces to play dreidel.

Facts about Dreidel

Dreidel is a traditional Hanukkah game that is like spinning a top. When put together, the Hebrew letters on the dreidel mean "Nes gadol haya sham," or "A great miracle happened there!" Dreidel is often played with gelt, the Hebrew word for money.

Shin

Hey

Gimmel

Nun

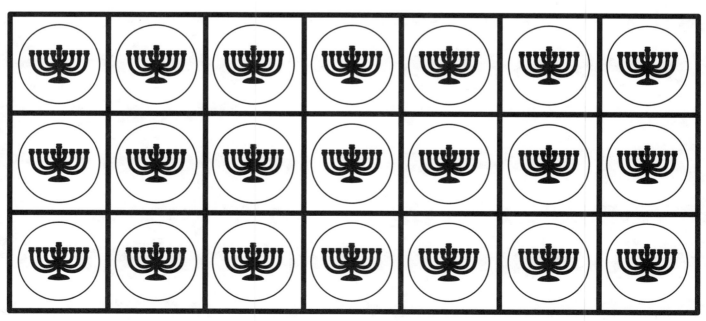

Make and share these thoughtful Hanukkah gifts.

Star of David Picture Frame

Gather 12 craft sticks, construction paper, a favorite picture, and glue. Place 2 craft sticks side-by-side on top of 2 others, overlapping and gluing the ends. Repeat this step to form a triangle. Make another triangle from the remaining sticks. Glue one triangle on top of the other to create a Star of David. Cut construction paper to fit the opening in the center. Glue a photograph to the paper, then glue the edges to the back of the frame. Glue yarn to the top for hanging.

Happy Hanukkah Card

Cut two large triangles from yellow paper. Outline the edges of the triangles with glue, then add gold glitter. Once dry, turn one triangle upside-down. Use clear tape to attach one triangle edge to the other triangle to form a Star of David. Decorate the top triangle with Hanukkah pictures. On the bottom triangle, write a Happy Hanukkah message.

Celebrate Hanukkah with these traditional foods.

Sufganiyot

Sufganiyot are jelly doughnuts sprinkled with sugar. They are often given to children as Hanukkah treats. Cut doughnut holes in half and spread a small amount of your favorite jelly on one side of each doughnut. Put the doughnut halves back together and then sprinkle with powdered sugar. Enjoy!

Latkes

Latkes are traditional potato pancakes fried in oil to recall the Hanukkah oil lamp miracle. Mix 2 pounds of grated potatoes and 1 medium grated onion. Add 1 egg, $3/4$ teaspoon salt, $1/4$ teaspoon pepper, and 1 tablespoon matzo meal or flour. Drop the mixture by spoonfuls onto a hot, well-oiled skillet and flatten into pancakes. Fry both sides until golden brown and drain off the vegetable oil. Serve warm with applesauce or sour cream.

Use the word list below to solve the Hanukkah crossword puzzle.

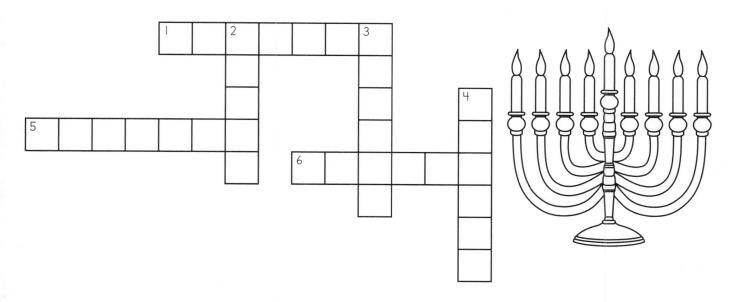

Word List

DREIDEL   KISLEV   LIGHTS
EIGHT   LATKES   MENORAH

Across

1. A _____ is a four-sided top marked with Hebrew letters. It is used to play a traditional game.
5. The _____ is a nine-branched candle holder lit during Hanukkah.
6. Traditional potato pancakes fried in oil are called _____.

Down

2. The menorah miraculously burned for _____ days.
3. Hanukkah is also known as "The Festival of _____."
4. Hanukkah begins on the twenty-fifth day of this Hebrew month.

Connect the dots to reveal a symbol of the Jewish faith. Start at the ★.

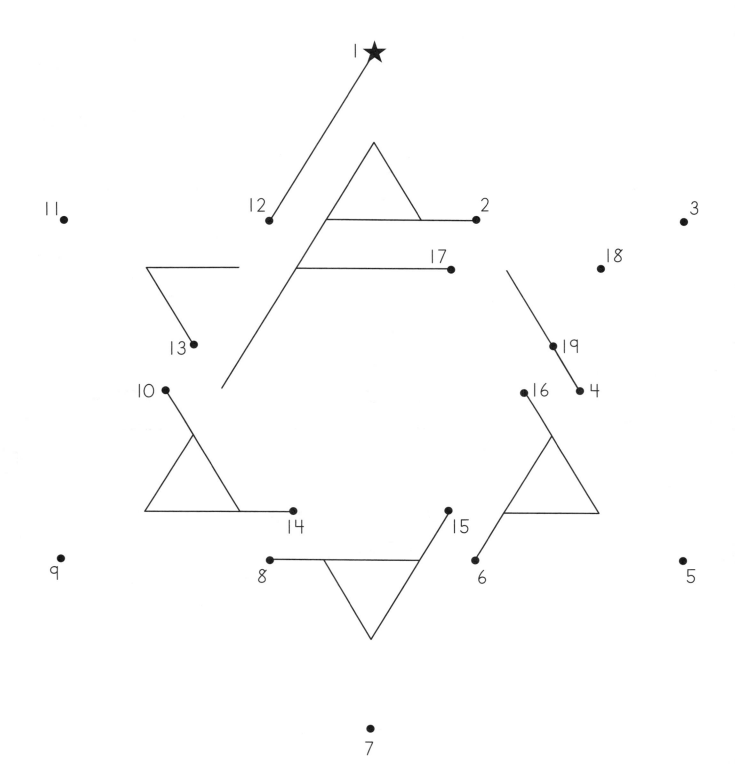

Christmas

December 25 is celebrated as the birthday of Jesus Christ. The events surrounding the Nativity (the birth of Jesus) are told in the Bible. Retelling these stories is an important part of many traditional Christmas celebrations. According to the gospel of Luke, an angel appeared to shepherds near the town of Bethlehem, telling them of Jesus' birth. The gospel of Matthew tells the story of the Magi, or wise men, who followed a bright and shining star to find the child Jesus.

During the Christmas season, many people decorate their homes with lights and evergreen Christmas trees. Families gather to sing songs, enjoy special holiday meals, attend religious ceremonies, and exchange gifts.

Who brought good news to the shepherds? Connect the dots to find out. Start at the ★. Color the picture.

Help the Magi follow the star to Bethlehem.

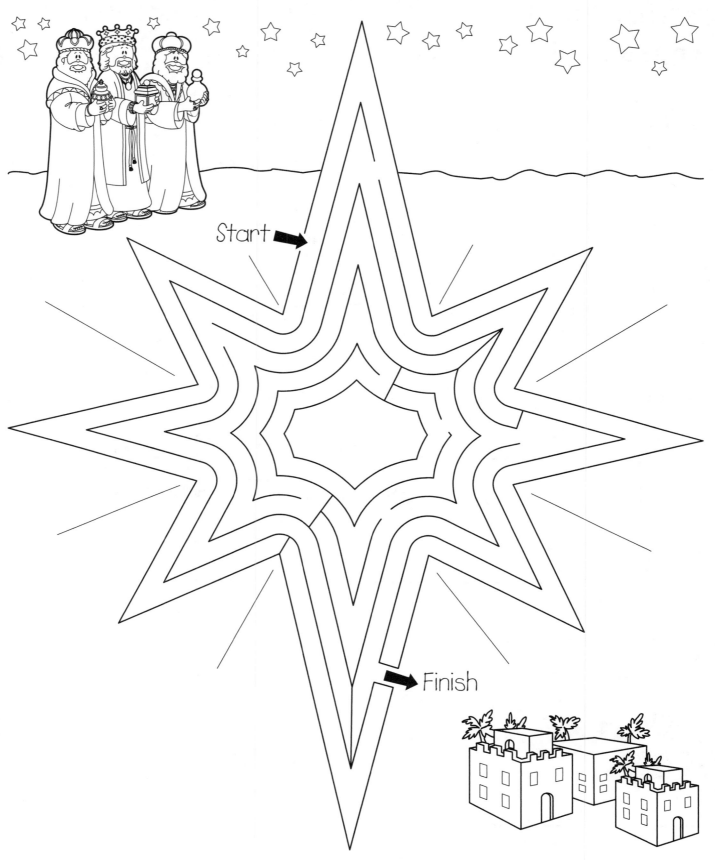

Start ➤

➤ Finish

Cross out the letters B, F, M, and U. Write the remaining letters in the blanks below to discover what the angels said to the shepherds in the fields.

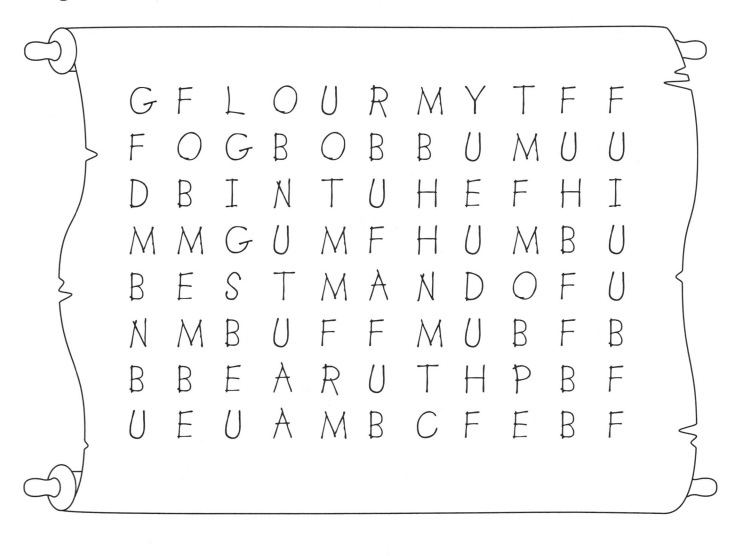

G F L O U R M Y T F F
F O G B O B B U M U U
D B I N T U H E F H I
M M G U M F H U M B U
B E S T M A N D O F U
N M B U F F M U B F B
B B E A R U T H P B F
U E U A M B C F E B F

"_____ ___ ___ ____ ___

___ _____ _____, ____ ___

___ _____ _____ . . ."

© Carson-Dellosa CD-0184 p. 12   (Luke 2:14)

How many words can you make from the letters in these words?

MERRY CHRISTMAS

1. _____
2. _____
3. _____
4. _____
5. _____
6. _____
7. _____
8. _____
9. _____
10. _____
11. _____
12. _____
13. _____
14. _____
15. _____
16. _____

17. _____
18. _____
19. _____
20. _____
21. _____
22. _____
23. _____
24. _____
25. _____
26. _____
27. _____
28. _____
29. _____
30. _____

Find and circle the Christmas words from the word list below.

```
M  Z  O  U  G  W  S  H  E  P  H  E  R  D  S
N  A  Y  M  C  V  H  K  G  J  C  S  T  A  R
A  K  G  S  R  D  U  G  D  I  Y  R  S  R
T  Y  E  I  A  C  G  I  T  Z  H  H  U  E  S
I  X  R  S  B  N  Y  G  M  S  J  S  G  A  Z
V  A  J  T  P  E  G  J  S  U  E  N  M  E  Z
I  B  O  W  C  F  T  E  N  J  A  T  M  S  Z
T  L  S  N  C  Z  N  H  L  M  S  J  K  Q  U
Y  M  E  N  I  L  X  G  L  I  D  W  F  X  L
U  R  P  E  Z  Y  L  H  R  E  G  N  M  F  X
M  E  H  R  M  N  E  H  M  W  H  I  E  Y  I
K  I  E  W  Y  L  C  J  U  K  I  E  F  I  U
V  Z  S  R  B  W  L  P  B  N  Z  P  M  T  M
S  M  A  T  G  K  N  D  Y  U  P  W  K  B  S
J  M  B  R  O  Y  K  C  F  O  F  W  I  X  Q
```

Word List

ANGEL   GIFTS   MAGI   NATIVITY
BETHLEHEM   JESUS   MANGER   SHEPHERDS
CHRISTMAS   JOSEPH   MARY   STAR

Color and cut out this Christmas card. Write a holiday message on the inside. Give the card to someone special.

© Carson-Dellosa CD-0184

KWANZAA

Kwanzaa is a seven-day holiday during which African-Americans celebrate African traditions and culture and strengthen family and community relationships. Many Kwanzaa activities are based on traditional African harvest festivals. During Kwanzaa, families gather to sing, dance, exchange gifts, give thanks, and remember their ancestors. There are seven principles, or main ideas, of Kwanzaa, and seven major symbols of the holiday.

Seven Principles of Kwanzaa

- Umoja .... Unity
- Kujichagulia .... Independence
- Ujima ....Community
- Ujamaa ....Cooperation
- Nia .... Purpose
- Kuumba .... Creativity
- Imani .... Faith

Seven Symbols of Kwanzaa

- Zawadi... gifts
- Mkeka .... woven mat
- Kikombe Cha Umoja .... unity cup
- Muhindi .... ears of corn
- Mazao .... harvest foods
- Kinara .... candle holder
- Mishumaa Saba .... seven candles

Enjoy these tasty Kwanzaa dishes with your family.

Harvest Fruit Salad

Gather 3 oranges, 3 apples, 3 pears, 1 1/2 cups seedless grapes, and 1 1/2 cups of orange juice. Have an adult help you peel and slice the oranges, apples, and pears. Place the fruit in a large bowl, then add the grapes and orange juice. Refrigerate until ready to serve. This recipe makes about 10 servings.

Black-Eyed Pea Salad

Have an adult help you rinse and drain two 16-ounce cans of black-eyed peas. In a large bowl, combine the peas, one medium chopped onion, two chopped stalks of celery, one seeded and chopped red bell pepper, and one bottle of vinaigrette salad dressing. Cover and refrigerate at least two hours. This recipe makes about 24 servings.

Find and circle the Seven Principles of Kwanzaa and their meanings from the word list below.

```
W F K U C O M M U N I T Y C I B C P U
F J E U J Z F W M O I O N X B I E I M
S Q H K U I S G J Q U K L D N S L D J
M T Z G U M M J O M W C Y A O E I F O
B H I N I J B A U V C A M P C C P S U
I C I D A M I A J Z I I R N M K F O J
D R O Y E Y D C B N E U E G W L C F B
W E G L S Z W H H N P D T B D P O P H
E A W M F R E D F A N J N T X G P V F
U T U O W J U I G E G Q F E C E X V G
Y I Z K N Q Y M P K B U E U Z R S X P
A V C N Z A A E B R Q Y L F N B X L B
D I K X J A D F F Z M G S I A I K O F
S T X O M N S I Y C E B L G A I T X Y
X Y M A I X X R N O H I N L J P T Y N
V U J H J T V G R B Z X Y L I A M H R
E U C O O P E R A T I O N J U D X Q A
```

Word List

UMOJA	UNITY	NIA	PURPOSE
KUJICHAGULIA	INDEPENDENCE	KUUMBA	CREATIVITY
UJIMA	COMMUNITY	IMANI	FAITH
UJAMAA	COOPERATION		

Write the letter of each Kwanzaa symbol beside its name.

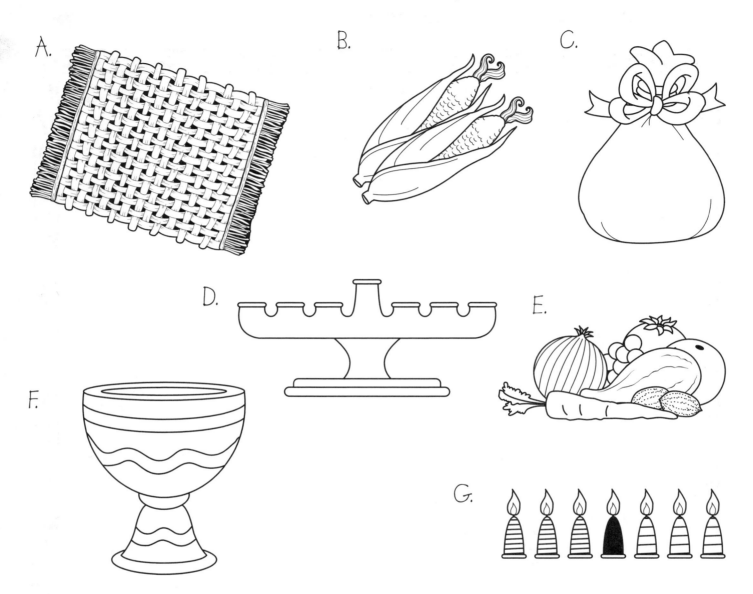

1. Mazao _____

2. Mkeka _____

3. Muhindi _____

4. Kinara _____

5. Zawadi _____

6. Kikombe Cha Umoja _____

7. Mishumaa Saba _____

Celebrate Kwanzaa with these useful, decorative crafts.

Make a Mkeka Mat

Fold a sheet of 8 1/2" x 11" black construction paper in half lengthwise. Make ten wavy cuts, about 1 inch apart, from the folded edge to 1 inch from the open edge. Unfold the paper. Use  crayons or markers to draw colorful designs on red and green construction paper. Cut the red and green paper lengthwise into 1" x 11" strips. One at a time, weave the strips over and under the black construction paper frame until the mkeka mat is complete. Weave straw or raffia into the mat to resemble dry grasses.

Kwanzaa Beaded Jewelry

Follow the instructions to make a batch of self-hardening salt dough. Make beads of various shapes and sizes. Use a toothpick or straw to make a hole in the center of each bead. Let the beads dry overnight, then paint them with tempera or acrylic paint. String the finished beads on a length of yarn, string, or natural raffia. Knot the ends together to make a necklace.

Self-Hardening Salt Dough

Mix 2 cups flour and 3/4 cup salt. Stir in 3/4 cup water, then knead the dough well. Add water if the mixture is too crumbly. Add flour if the mixture is too sticky. Dough will harden if left exposed, or can be baked at 300° for 30–40 minutes.

Circle the letter under the correct heading for each Kwanzaa word. Write the circled letters in the blanks below to learn the name of the creator of Kwanzaa.

Kwanzaa Words	Principle	Symbol
1. IMANI	M	A
2. KIKOMBE CHA UMOJA	N	A
3. KINARA	A	U
4. KUJICHAGULIA	L	I
5. KUUMBA	A	E
6. MAZAO	S	N
7. MISHUMAA SABA	U	A
8. MKEKA	S	K
9. MUHINDI	E	A
10. NIA	R	F
11. UJAMAA	E	F
12. UJIMA	N	A
13. UMOJA	G	A
14. ZAWADI	T	A

Dr. __ __ __ __ __ __ __ __

__ __ __ __ __ __ __

Find and circle the **8** differences between these two Kwanzaa scenes.

New Year

People of almost every nationality, culture, and religion celebrate the New Year, but not always at the same time! In the United States, Canada, England, Australia, and throughout much of Europe and Latin America, New Year's Day is celebrated January 1 of each year. On New Year's Eve, December 31, families and friends gather to remember the past and look forward to the future. People wear party hats, eat, sing, and dance. When the clock strikes midnight on New Year's Eve, people ring bells, blow noisemakers and whistles, and watch fireworks displays. It is a time of great hope, celebration, and reflection. On New Year's Day, many people eat special meals that are supposed to bring health, happiness, wealth, and luck for the coming year.

Ring in the New Year with these fun and easy crafts.

New Year Time Capsule

Think about your hopes and dreams for the coming year. On notebook paper, write some things you hope will happen during the new year. Roll the paper into a tube and place it in a clean, dry, plastic soda bottle. Tighten and glue the lid in place. Keep the bottle sealed in a safe place. In one year, open the time capsule and see if your dreams have come true.

New Year's Eve Party Hats

Roll a large piece of colorful construction paper into a cone shape. Trim off the extra paper and unroll the cone. Decorate the paper with crayons or markers. Roll the paper back into a cone. Tape the edges of the paper together along the inside seam. To make a chin strap, punch holes in the base of the hat and tie elastic cord or string between the holes.

Draw lines to match the New Year's hats that are the same. Color each pair of matching hats the same.

Help Baby New Year get to Father Time!

Start

Finish

Chinese New Year

The Chinese New Year usually arrives between January 20 and February 19, and lasts for fifteen days. People clean their houses to sweep away bad luck, decorate with red, the color of luck and happiness, and give packets of coins to children and poor people. On the fifteenth day of the new year, families hang beautiful lanterns around their houses and gardens, and in the streets and temples. Parades and fireworks are a major part of every Chinese New Year celebration. Dancers dress up as dragons and lions.

The Chinese New Year is also a time for celebrating birthdays. No matter what time of year people were born, everyone turns a year older during New Year. Each year of the Chinese calendar is symbolized by one of twelve animals, and people are often said to possess the traits of their animal symbol.

Color by number to see a Chinese symbol of good luck, goodness, and strength.

1 = purple   2 = yellow   3 = blue   4 = red

Make and display these Chinese New Year crafts.

Chinese Paper Lantern

Draw decorative designs on a piece of colorful construction paper using crayons or markers. Fold the paper lengthwise. Beginning at the fold, carefully make cuts one inch apart, ending one inch from the open edge of the paper. Unfold the paper and roll it into a tube. Tape or staple along the edge to secure the paper. To hang the lantern, make two holes at the top, then tie a piece of string through the holes.

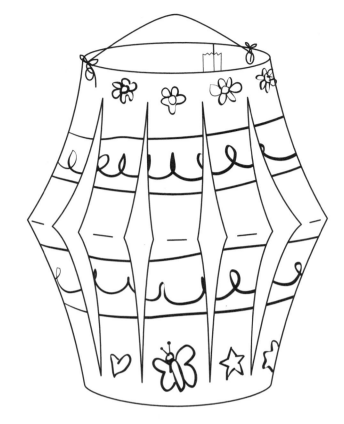

Lucky Door Hanger

Roll each end of a piece of red construction paper around a cardboard tube or other small cylinder, and tape the edges to secure them. Use a black marker to draw the good luck symbol at left and write good luck messages on the flat space between the tubes. Thread a piece of string or yarn through the top tube and tie it together. Hang the scroll for good luck.

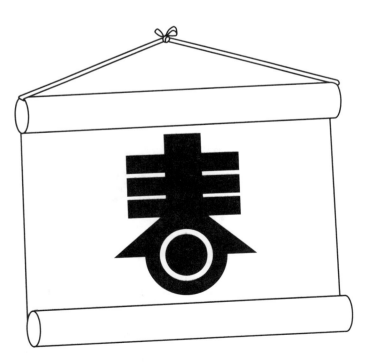

Do you know your Chinese zodiac sign? Find the year you were born on the chart below, then look at the year's animal traits. Are you like your animal symbol? Color and cut out the zodiac wheel and share it with your family and friends.

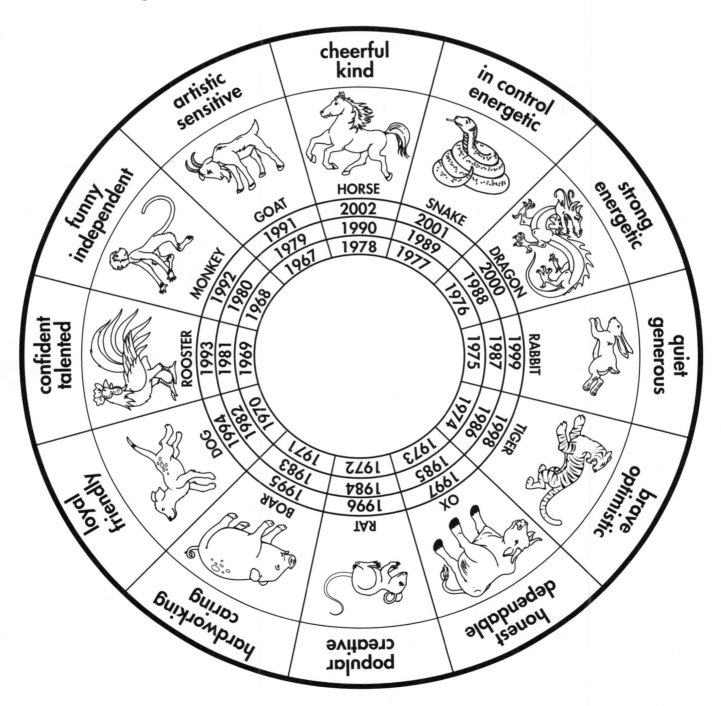

Use the word list to answer these winter holiday riddles.

Word List

Chinese New Year   Hanukkah   New Year

Christmas   Kwanzaa

---

1. Fireworks and lanterns and lucky red treats,
   Dragons and lions dance in the streets.

   _____

2. Latkes and dreidels and oil for eight nights,
   Light the menorah for the "Festival of Lights."

   _____

3. Waiting for midnight with hope and good cheer,
   We gather with friends to say, "Happy ____ ____!"

   _____

4. "First fruits" and family and African ways,
   We recall Seven Principles on these seven days.

   _____

5. An angel appeared to shepherds on earth
   To announce the good news of Jesus' birth.

   _____